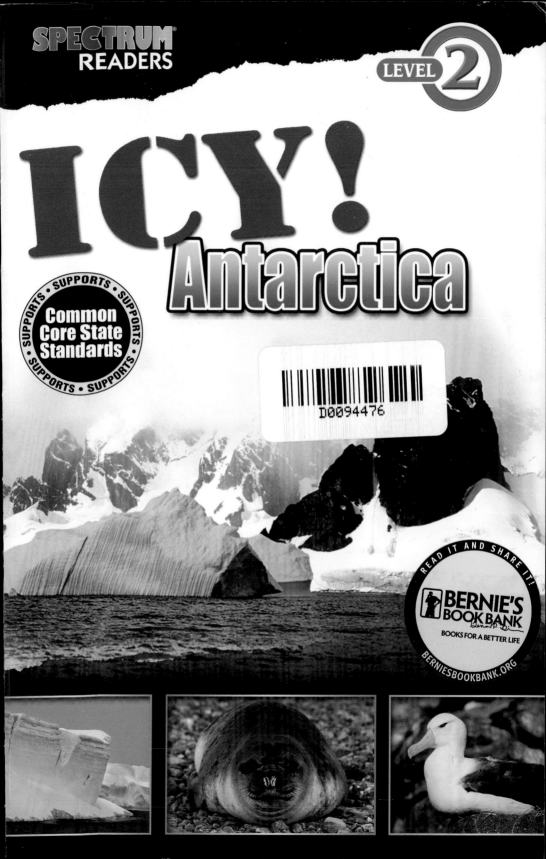

SPECTRUM READERS

LEVEL 2

ICY!
Antarctica

D0094476

Dear Parents,
  Spectrum Readers are the perfect way to introduce your child to nonfiction text, which is important to becoming a good reader.
  In Level 2, Emerging Readers are introduced to a greater range of age-appropriate vocabulary. The high-interest topics are presented using slightly longer sentences that allow your child to advance his or her reading skills. Repetitive language will give your child lots of practice with new words.
  Here are some ways you can help your child be a successful reader:

- Demonstrate how to sound out new words by pointing to individual letters and making the sounds. Then, blend the sounds together.

- When you come to a difficult word, point to a picture clue that will help your child identify the word and its meaning.

- Ask lots of questions while you are reading to invite discussion and language development.

- Be sure to read the book many, many times to build reading fluency and confidence.

SPECTRUM®
READERS

LEVEL 2

ICY!
Antarctica

By Lisa Kurkov

Carson-Dellosa
Publishing

SPECTRUM®

An imprint of Carson-Dellosa Publishing, LLC
P.O. Box 35665
Greensboro, NC 27425-5665

carsondellosa.com

Printed in the USA. All rights reserved.
ISBN 978-1-4838-0120-9

01-002141120

Head south.
Don't stop until you get to the South
Pole, at the bottom of the planet.
You are in Antarctica!
No one lives here full time.
No trees or bushes grow here.
The sun rises and sets only once a year.
Life is different in Antarctica.

Antarctic Facts

Antarctica is the coldest and windiest place on Earth.

It can reach 128°F below zero!

Antarctica is the fifth largest continent, yet it does not have a single city.

It has no official language, and no country controls it.

Snow

Antarctica is a snowy place.
It is also a desert.
Antarctica gets only about two inches
of snow each year.
The snow is old, and it never melts.
Layers of snow build up over time.

Ice

Antarctica is covered in ice.
The ice can be a mile thick!
Most of Earth's ice is found on the
continent of Antarctica.
The ocean surrounding Antarctica is
full of icebergs.
They make travel by water difficult!

Emperor Penguin

Antarctica is home to emperor penguins.

They huddle together for protection from cold and wind.

They take turns standing in the middle of the group, where it is warmer.

Fathers keep the eggs safe while mothers hunt for food.

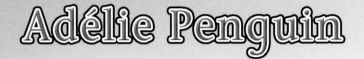

Adélie Penguin

Antarctica is home to Adélie penguins.
They weigh only about 10 pounds.
They are good swimmers and can dive
almost 600 feet under water!
They build nests made of rocks.
Parents take turns sitting on the eggs.

13

Krill

Antarctica is home to sea animals called *krill*.
Krill look like small shrimp.
They are tiny, but very important.
Most Antarctic animals rely on krill as a food source.
At times, huge swarms of krill can be spotted from space!

Humpback Whale

Antarctica is home to humpback whales.
They spend the summer months in Antarctic waters.
These whales can be 50 feet long.
During their time in Antarctica, they eat a lot of krill!
In the winter, they migrate to warmer waters.

Weddell Seal

Antarctica is home to Weddell seals.
They swim and dive in icy waters.
They spend a lot of time below the ice!
Weddell seals find tasty fish to eat in
deep waters.
They must come up for air every
45 minutes.

Crabeater Seal

Antarctica is home to crabeater seals.
They don't really eat crabs.
Like many other Antarctic animals,
they eat krill!
They dive for five minutes at a time.
Crabeater seals must watch out for
killer whales.
These giant predators are a major
threat.

Cape Petrel

Antarctica is home to Cape petrels. Like penguins, they are black and white in color.

They lay only one egg at a time, but may not recognize their own eggs. Sometimes, Cape petrel parents raise other birds' chicks!

Cape petrels spend the winter in Australia.

Albatross

Antarctica is home to the albatross. This seabird has an amazing wingspan—11 feet wide! Albatrosses glide on air currents. They can go for a long time without flapping their wings. They spend most of their time at sea.

Research

Antarctica is a place for scientists to do research.

Because the weather is so harsh, most don't stay long.

Scientists study icebergs and glaciers, which are masses of slowly moving ice.

Scientists study Antarctic animals, too.

Tourism

Antarctica is a place tourists like to visit and explore.

About 40,000 people visit each year.

Most come on cruise ships.

There is no other place like Antarctica.

Tourists must help protect it.

They should leave no trace behind.

Mystery

Antarctica is a cold and lonely place.
It can be beautiful, too.
The continent has changed little in
thousands of years.
In many ways, it is still a mystery.
What secrets do the layers of snow and
ice hold?

ICY! Antarctica
Comprehension Questions

1. How many people live all year in Antarctica?

2. Why is Antarctica a desert?

3. On what continent is most of Earth's ice found?

4. What is the role of emperor penguin fathers?

5. What are krill?

6. Name two animals that eat krill.

7. When do humpback whales live in Antarctica?

8. What animal is a threat to crabeater seals?

9. Where does an albatross spend most of its time?

10. What do scientists study in Antarctica?